KNOW HOW TO
CONNECT

How a Name Can Predict Communication Styles

by

SHARÓN LYNN WYETH

Published by

L|ghtKeepers

Iowa City, Iowa * San Diego, California * Redlands, California * Arcadia, California *Neu-brücke, Germany * San Antonio, Texas * Tokyo, Japan * Lincoln, Nebraska * Roswell, New Mexico * Beaverton, Oregon * Longview, Washington * Shanghai, China * Crockett, Texas * Leon Valley, Texas * Hailey, Idaho * Boca Raton, Florida * Kingsport, Tennessee

DEDICATION

This book is dedicated to those individuals who have curious minds and who wish to be able to communicate more clearly with other people in order to establish rapport rapidly. Neimology® Science is the study of the placement of the letters in someone's name, which then enables us to better understand others at a deeper level simply by knowing their name. This knowledge is immediately available, as our names are related to how we think, feel, and act. Neimology® Science is most useful in helping individuals interpret the clues that other people send. In turn, this saves time and energy in the complicated task of getting to understand another person. Neimology® Science assists us in acquiring a new set of skills in comprehending how other people function in this world. Essentially, each name holds a key to a person's talents and gifts, and at the same time, identifies one's challenges to be faced in this lifetime. Welcome to a new path of understanding and discovery.

Each individual is born into this life with both talents and challenges. Talents help the person learn and grow which can provide gifts for the rest of the world. Challenges provide a testing ground in order for the person to become strong and resilient and have more compassion for others. Every person born has something to contribute to our world as gifts, and each has multiple challenges to overcome. Therefore, it is my desire that we not use Neimology® Science to judge someone but rather to assist him or her, just as we also wish not to be judged.

Without the help of the following people, this book would not have happened: Meg Chojnacki (editor and grammar queen), Dr. Stacy Reddan (print manuscript style), Don Cole (cover design), and Jovanna Robinson-Delahay (book formatting).

TABLE OF CONTENTS

INTRODUCTION

This book expands a minuscule part of the entire Neimology® Science system. It focuses on the first vowel in the first name because that is where our communication style is located within a name.

Do we become our name or does our name become us? Often, it is some of both. Names definitely have an effect on the people who bear them. Analyzing our names via Neimology® Science is utilizing one more tool which can be used to demonstrate to our psyches that our lives were not randomly or chaotically planned but have a systematic structure. There was an ordered design, revealed in our names, that clarifies our life's purpose. Although a name gives many aspects of one's personality, it does not mean one is stuck with the traits assigned to his or her name as once you understand the design within your name, you are better able to alter the effect of your name on you.

By understanding the component letters in names and the characteristics they endow, one can affect change by means of knowledge. A person can always choose to change any self-defining trait or quality. Just as habits can be altered with conscious intention, characteristics and qualities in a name can also be changed.

Not all of the traits assigned to a name will be present at birth to the same extent that they will exist later in life. One would not expect the same dominating personality characteristics to be present in a five-year-old as in a fifty-year-old. It is no different with names; the same attribute is still present, but is frequently altered by life experience, age, and good or bad judgment.

According to Donald Duck in Disney's video "Donald

Duck in Mathemagic Land," mathematics is the language of the Universe. What makes a good mathematician is the ability to see patterns. Life is full of patterns that repeat themselves at various times to see if we have grown to the next level. Neimology® Science identifies the patterns that appear in names just as clearly as mathematicians identify the patterns in a mathematical algorithm. Our names are a preview to the patterns that will show themselves throughout our lives. If we know how to read our names, we can better determine how to master those patterns instead of having them dominate us.

People always ask others for their names. When asked who you are, we answer with our name as if that says it all. It does indeed once you know how to decipher a name utilizing Neimology® Science. What most people do not realize is that they have just revealed who they are once they have replied with their names. From that point on, a person is treated by how others perceive that person to be, based on their name, and the previous encounters with others who have similar names. Realize that once you have provided your full name to anyone who understands Neimology® Science, you are now, to some extent, exposed. Merely providing the first name gives far more information than many realize, even though it takes the entire name to decipher a name accurately. It is important to realize that all names shine light on who a person really is. However, it is more important what one does with their name than what the actual name conveys.

Why are our names the key? Various groups throughout history have understood the importance of names, and ancient cultures all gave value to the importance of names. For example, in the book of Genesis in the Bible, Abram and Sarai's names are changed to Abraham and Sarah, now giving each an 'AH' combination. Neimology® Science indicates that the 'AH' is representative of being on mission for the Divine, and immediately after being renamed both Abraham and Sarah did start their missions. Each faith has a way of placing importance on names. Neimology® Science identifies the patterns in names so that these ancient systems are rediscovered. Thus, instead of going to a book and looking up what a name means and reading a few words, you have the information needed to interpret the entire name and all that a name reveals. This book gives a small glimpse into the knowledge that is hidden within the name as it relates to the basics of a relationship. The complete system is available for you to learn if interested.

Why does analyzing names work? There are two suppositions. First, according to Dr. Eugene Whitworth's research[1], there was a time when there were only seven religions in the world, before I jokingly say that they multiplied, divided, and everyone made up their own. Those seven religions were based on the Zohar, and thus, they agreed on the same basic information since it derived from the same source. One of those beliefs mentioned in the Zohar was that the incoming soul impresses upon the one naming them what the soul wishes to be called. So, in essence, we name ourselves. Thus, it would make sense that our name fits us.

Now let's look at the scientific reason why Neimology® Science works. Let me quote David Tame[2] in his book, <u>The Secret Power of Music</u>, where he states "Is DNA influenced

---

1   Dr. Eugene Whitworth authored six spiritual books, including the bestselling Nine Faces of Christ, and founded Western University in the San Francisco Bay area in California.
2   The Secret Power of Music: The Transformation of Self and Society Through Musical Energy: The Transformation of Self and Society Through Musical Energy by David Tame (18-Apr-1984)

by the Spoken Word? They found that the alkaline of our DNA follow regular grammar and have set rules just like spoken languages. The implication seems to be that human languages have not appeared randomly but are, in fact, a reflection of our inherent DNA. The scientists managed, for example, to modulate certain frequency patterns onto a laser ray and with it influenced the DNA frequency and thus the genetic information it contains." So, if the spoken language can influence our DNA, why not the language that we identify with the most, our names?

Then there is the science of Cymatics. "Cymatics is the study of the physical impacts of sound which demonstrates that sounds create visible geometries. Medical research has proven that cell structures, neurological systems, and the body generally responds directly to sound. It shows that repetition of sounds can create or ameliorate disease. Making a connection between behavior associated to the oft-heard name and cellular responses proven in hard science is not an untenable leap." [3] So, names affect our cellular structure.[4]

Sharry Edward[5] was named Scientist of the year in 2001 by the International Association for new science for her research and work in bioacoustics (sound) Biology when AT&T declared that bioacoustics is the "medicine of the future." Bioacoustics indicates how sound can be used to heal. Edwards' has made incredible progress identifying how sound can change DNA. More and more, scientists are realizing the importance of a name. Another example of this is the quantum bio feedback machine which uses a mathematical vector to determine the status of a physical body. One of the three points needed to create the vector is our name!

3   Review on Amazon by Old Soul for Know the Name; Know the Person
4   This is explored more in Know the Name; Know the Health
5   More information can be found at soundhealthoptions.com

Today's scientists are catching up with what we see in very ancient texts when understanding the importance behind a name was considered common knowledge. Everybody knew names revealed the magic behind our lives if one only knew how to read the name. Thus, it appears that various sciences are now discovering the connection between sound with the most important sound, that of our names and our DNA. When someone asks us, "Who are you?" we answer with our name as if that says it all. Indeed it does, once you know how to interpret a name utilizing Neimology® Science.

CHAPTER ONE

"Beloved. I call you by your name, for only then will you know the truth about yourself."
     The Art of Spiritual Peacemaking by James Twyman

In Neimology® Science, the first vowel in the first name characterizes the main elements of how one thinks, feels, and behaves. The first vowel is the dominant characteristic in the name and carries the most weight when compared to the remaining letters in the first name. This vowel does not have the same meaning when it appears elsewhere in the name. For an example, compare the 'A' described below where it is the first vowel in the name with the 'A' in the middle of the name which reflects not wanting to do any more work than what is necessary. 'A' in the last letter of the first name indicates the person's desire to be liked.

Much can be assessed from the first vowel, and if only this one aspect is remembered, this information alone can help in better understanding and communicating with other people. Thus, this book will expand on what has been stated in the book, "Know the Name; Know the Person". The definitions of each letter reveal the dominant points; however, each letter is influenced by the other letters in the name and so each characteristic can be made stronger or weaker depending on other letters and their placement. Remember the most dominant trait in the first name is the first vowel.

ALL VOWELS PRESENT IN A NAME

There are four positions that a letter can hold in a name. The letter can be the first vowel, seen in the name when reading the name from left to right, the first letter, the last letter and the rest are the middle letters. The first vowel in the name yields more information than any other letter or position in the name. The first vowel tells how one thinks and behaves; what type of gifts they prefer to receive; and whether they have any idiosyncrasies. The first vowel in the name is the main letter to know as it produces the fastest amount of information. Each of the letters in a name influence the interpretation of the other letters; however, the first vowel is the least influenced by other letters and affects the other letters the most. An interesting sidebar is that person is a jack-of-all-trades when his or her full name contains all of the vowels.

WHAT THIS BOOK CONTAINS

This is but a small indication of what is indicated by your name as your name reveals how you think, feel and behave. An in-depth analysis reveals the blueprint and timing for your entire life, the seven lessons that you came to master, and the overall theme of your life: the reason why you are here. Your name indicates your multiple talents as well as how to develop and utilize them to your fullest potential.

Your name also indicates your way of learning, the types of presents you enjoy receiving, and where potential conflicts with others would more than likely occur. Your name indicates so many things, from what you like in the bedroom to how you know if you are loved or not, even what causes you to want to shut down and quit. The best part is that even solutions to your challenges can be found in your name. This book shares a small, yet highly significant, sampling of what is hidden in your name.

CHAPTER TWO: FIRST VOWEL IS 'A'

"Thoughts lead to and create our feelings; it's not the other way around."
Might of the Thoughts by Eduard Albert Meier

People with the first vowel of 'A' desire honesty, truth, justice, wisdom, and are self-reliant and detail oriented. When these individuals work, they work hard and tend to be considered workaholics. However, when they play, they can be incredibly lazy. 'A's are one of the two vowels that have an easy time multitasking.

These are the dependable and reliable people in an organization. They see what others have forgotten to do and follow through for them because they are detail orientated and want the group to look good. 'A' people do not realize that if someone does not see that a task needs to be done, they are also not going to be aware that it has been completed. Consequently 'A's are often surprised when no gratitude is expressed. However, 'A's crave praise and continue to complete the tasks others forget even while feeling unappreciated. Think of Martha and her quiet service in Biblical times.

The typical 'A' person will self-sacrifice for the good of the whole organization or group. It is often a challenge for

the 'A' is to balance their tendency to be overly self-sacrific-
ing with their feelings; thus, others take advantage of them.
'A's sacrifice to their own detriment unless there is a double
'N' in the name, a 'B' at the beginning of the name or a 'BR'
somewhere in the forename. Therefore, a challenge that the
'A' person has is to make and keep clear, precise boundaries.
Mary Magdalene typifies this ability to stay focused, while
driven with purpose, and continually self-sacrificing.

In contrast the 'A' can overindulge in any area that they
really like. For example, if the 'A' really enjoys chocolate, 'A'
will be unable or unwilling to let the chocolate sit for very
long before eating the entire amount. This amounts to the
'A's having cravings with which they attempt to satisfy their
appetite. Excessive self-indulgence is not limited to food.
Most 'A's express this tendency in the number of books that
they own and read. However, the need for extravagance can
appear in any category, and so these practical people look
impractical in their area of overindulgence, be it art projects,
books, candy or simply the number of friends they have.

The first vowel of an 'A' denotes individuals that are
hardworking and do a great job, but who, if they make even
one error, judge themselves a harshly. The 'A' person thrives
on sincere compliments from those with whom they interact. Consequently, they do their best to keep working hard
so that the compliments keep coming. However, when criticized by others, they want to shut down and quit. Anything
that implies or can be interpreted as saying to an 'A' that
they somehow are not good enough causes them to want to
not attempt whatever they are doing again.

The 'A' person becomes resentful when others get credit
for their work. They have learned that everything they do
will not get recognition; however, it hurts them deeply to see

someone else getting credit for their efforts. Remember the absolute fits that Bart Simpson exhibits when this happens to him on the Simpson cartoon show?

'A's react more favorably to an approach which emphasizes the positive versus criticism, since the 'A' person aims to please others. 'A's respond when approached in a constructive manner: for example; "I always like it when you put the dishes away" versus "Why didn't you put the dishes away"? To extend this example, suppose a person with the first vowel 'A' is loading the dishwasher and you tell let the person that the way the dishwasher is being loaded will make it necessary to run the dishwasher more than one time for that particular meal. All the 'A' will hear is that s/he is not good enough because s/he can't even load the dishwasher correctly. Thus, the 'A's response prior to walking away would be, "Since you know how you want the dishwasher loaded, you load it!" Good luck getting the 'A' to load the dishwasher again.

However, if instead of insinuating that 'A' wasn't loading the dishwasher correctly, you said, "I wonder if there is a way to load this dishwasher so that all of the dishes got clean and they would all fit in such a way that we would only need to run the dishwasher once? What do you think?" The 'A' person would find this a challenge. So 'A' would look forward to loading the dishwasher each time because loading the dishwasher is now a puzzle that needs to be solved.

In other words, you can say whatever you like to an 'A'. You just have to know how to say it because 'A's can be overly sensitive. Thus, make suggestions to an 'A' and avoid giving direct corrections. This sensitivity often carries over to others as 'A's usually notice when another person's feelings are hurt. If 'A' is the culprit, 'A' will do his best to make amends unless the 'A' felt that you were being rude and deserve the smart remarks.

Remember that 'A's are very observant, don't miss much, even as they don't share even half of what they notice. In fact, 'A's will notice around ninety-four percent of what is happening around them during the day, whereas others on average may notice as little as fifty percent. However, when 'A' realizes that something was missed, the 'A' person beats himself up, wondering what happened that he missed the remaining six percent. The 'A' says to himself, what needs to change so that the six percent isn't missed again? What needs to happen differently so that the six percent is noticed? Ideally the 'A' persona would celebrate observing the ninety-four percent instead of focusing so much on the six percent missed.

Stating things in the negative often brings up the 'A's rebellious streak. Once ignited, this rebelliousness has a tendency to bleed over into other areas and can show up as a tendency to take things to the extreme. 'A's combat self-doubt, self-criticism, , and their own insecurity. Occasionally they will even combat self-sabotage in their quest to do well.

The 'A' person does not like to be told 'no' and will often seek alternative solutions to a problem. They also can become quite insistent upon a different solution when authority appears unjust or unreasonable in any way. This is when you'll see the 'A's persistence as often 'A' will ask the same thing in multiple different ways, attempting to get a 'yes' response.

The 'A' persona enjoys competency in self and others and usually lacks tolerance for incompetence unless they realize that someone is just learning the skill. When the incompetence is in their boss, they slowly take over the organization to lead it themselves. However, they are happiest when working for a competent person because they enjoy being the power behind others and prefer to avoid the limelight. 'A's wish to be helpful. Remember, they work for praise more than money.

Often others consider the 'A' to be a workaholic. However, at the end of the day, 'A's make great couch potatoes. Consider 'A's as being like a battery; they will go and go and go, until their individual battery goes dead. Then they stop, just as quickly as a dead battery stops whatever it was powering. That is when they quit for the day, even wishing someone else could go to the bathroom for them as they don't want to get up for any reason. This may translate into not wanting to go to bed at night, simply because once down, the 'A' doesn't wish to move.

Due to their obsessiveness with work, each 'A's reach a point in their lives when they no longer want responsibility for anyone but themselves and tend to avoid taking on any new tasks until this need for solitude passes. This normally occurs somewhere between the mid-forties and mid-fifties. Since the 'A' has been busy accumulating responsibilities during the first part of life, they unload as much responsibility as possible once this point is reached. It is during this time 'A's would like to also not be responsible for self, especially if they think they could get away with it. Given a few non-responsible years, most 'A's will once again accumulate responsibilities, only this time they will be responsible for themselves and to others instead of attempting to be responsible for everyone around them.

Dan Rather is a superb example of the typical 'A' personality. Look at how people love to hear him. What is that

'A' saying to you via Dan Rather? He exemplifies truth, wisdom, salt of the Earth, and we know we are going to get the real story from him. We are going to trust what he says, because he will search for the truth. There have been quite a few times Dan Rather has put his job on the line to make sure that truth came out and that no one changed any part of his report. He is a workaholic by everyone's definition. He sets high standards for himself because nothing less than his best would be acceptable.

Immediately prior to his retirement, there was an incident about breaking a news story where the facts had not been adequately double-checked. Dan Rather may have been in too big of a hurry to release a scoop. 'A's hold their reputations and work ethics in high regard. Being a typical 'A', Dan would have wanted to have a flawless record, so that this error, especially so close to his retirement, must have really devastated him. Even if his retirement had not already been planned, this type of mistake is what influences 'A's to want to quit. Notice how quickly Dan Rather publicly apologized. In typical 'A' fashion, once an error has been made, rectifications must be made immediately.

The 'A' personality approaches life from a mental perspective, as such, 'A's need private time to be alone. Often times they wish that they could just bypass feelings as feelings are frequently unwieldy and need to be controlled. The 'A' persona dwells on situations only until mental understanding occurs. Then the situation is dismissed, and the 'A' person moves forward and overcomes the emotion.

Due to being mentally based, the 'A' personality appreciates gifts that are of a practical nature: something that can be used or art that is exquisite in some way. Frequently the 'A' personality will give away unwanted gifts, as they do not want unused items cluttering up the area. This aspect of the 'A' can be overridden by 'D's or 'F's in the name because D's benefit from having clutter around them and F's can become hoarders.

The 'A' person is usually spiritual or intuitive by nature. Normally the more 'A's in a name the more important spirituality is, as in Paramahansa Yogananda, the great Hindu yogi who is the main subject of <u>The Autobiography of a Yogi</u>. The 'ARA' combination also assists Yogananda as 'ARA' indicates intelligence at an early age, growing up rapidly and maturing at an early age. Since the 'A' person loves to learn, asking them what they have been reading lately is an easy way to start a conversation.

In dealing with someone who has the first vowel of an 'A' remember:

- These people are observant; they don't miss much
- Couch criticisms by suggesting a change, as they shut down when anything implies they are not good enough
- Ask them, do not tell them what to do, so as not to initiate their rebellious streak
- Thank or praise them for their efforts to encourage more of the same behavior
- Buy them practical gifts, as if not wanted or liked, they will give away what you got for them
- Remember that they want to please you, so be reasonable with your requests
- Balance their tendency to self-sacrifice with pitching in a helping hand

If you have the first vowel of 'A', remember:
- People do not see half of what you do, so do not expect acknowledgement or thanks for your efforts
- Learn to praise yourself
- Give yourself permission to say "no"
- Remember to build playtime or private time into each day

LEARNING STYLE

There are three main learning styles, visual, auditory and kinesthetic. The first vowel of 'A' indicates that the individual's primary way of learning is visual, with the secondary modality being auditory. Thus, when introducing the 'A' person to a new concept, it is best to provide a visual picture of the concept, and/or a one -page summary for the 'A' to read later. Remember, they are practical and if given too much material, they will think it's crazy to have to read that much when it can be condensed, so provide a brief summary. Being visual, the 'A' will take copious notes when interested in a subject as it helps their memory when they can refer to the notes later. Notes don't have to be written; they can be depicted in pictures, or other means, as visual aids assist the transfer of knowledge. 'A's generally tend to over-learn concepts as they can be so apprehensive on tests, that well-known material can escape them. Thus, it is best if an 'A' reviews material previous to any exam, or presentation.

LOVE LANGUAGE

Each vowel shows love differently. It is important to understand how the first vowel in the name shows love so that you understand how each vowel feels love. How one shows love is saying how one perceives they are loved. It is wisest to show another person love in the method that they understand the best, and to receive it in the manner that you understand it best. This is similar to when two people who are native speakers in different languages wish to clearly communicate, especially if neither is fluent in the other person's language yet knows some the language. The clearest communication takes place when one hears their native tongue and then speaks the other one's native language back to them. The same holds true for how we express love, our love language. If we can show love to others in the style that they can easily recognize then we are doing a better job of communicating our feelings.

So, 'A's typically show their love for you by helping you with your work load. In the 'A's way of thinking, it is a loving act to assist you in finishing your work earlier than expected as then you can relax sooner which is the desired goal. So, if you love a person whose first vowel is 'A' see where you can assist them with their work. They are most appreciative and recognize that you are saying, "I love you" when you take your time to help them. Also, recognize you are receiving love when an 'A' assists you with your work load or does some of your chores for you.

'A's are generally not overly wordy in expressing their love for another, almost never gushy about it, and usually are not fond of very much PDA, public displays of affection. So, other than holding their hand or putting your arm out for them to hold, don't expect much affection to be showed publicly. This does not mean that they are not affectionate people, just that they value their privacy and consider it respectful to not embarrass others or cause uncomfortable situations for others when demonstrating too much PDA.

COMMUNICATION STYLE

'A's are direct and appreciate getting to the point quickly. Long, elaborate stories try their patience. They often have so much work on their plate that they appreciate people giving summaries of information without elaborating on all of the details. If more specifics are needed, they will ask for them. Most 'A's, being sensitive to others, are tactful in what or how they say something as to avoid hurting another's feelings accidentally. However, tact is often missing when 'A' is both the first vowel in the name and also the first letter in the name as it then holds two key positions. 'A's appreciate getting their work done prior to playing and/or socializing.

So, don't be surprised when the person who has the first vowel of 'A' greets you with immediate talk of what work needs to be finished and doesn't inquire as to how you are feeling or if everything is okay with you. Once the work is completed 'A's show that they care how you are doing. Work generally comes first. Amazingly, 'A's are often the ones who come clean your house for you, bring you an extra meal, or take care of your pets if you are over wrought, sick, or needing assistance. 'A's like to get to the point and easily get annoyed when conversations degenerate into the mundane. It is most expedient to collect your thoughts prior to speaking to an 'A' and then to be concise in your conversations. Only once the work load is finished, do the 'A's relax, and allow themselves to play.

GIFT PREFERENCES

'A's enjoy items that are practical that can save them time or that assist them in learning something new. They can also appreciate something beautiful, yet they have their own particular taste which has been developed over time. Thus, choosing something that is a decorative for them is difficult as it has to fit perfectly within their own eclectic sense of style. The safest gift to give an 'A' is a gift certificate to either Amazon, or another bookstore, as they love to read and/or learn.

'A's have no qualms about re-gifting an item if it is not wanted or useful. Normally the 'A' is not into gadgets because they just take up more space, nor do they want items that need to be dusted unless the item is what they would consider a museum quality piece of art. Remember 'A's love to read, so a book is a good idea, but only if you are aware of what genre they read as just any book won't do.

HOW TO MAINTAIN A LONG RELATIONSHIP

'A's enjoy the company of friends who can teach them something and present to them different ideas that are well thought out and contain facts versus opinions. People with the first vowel of 'A' have little patience for stupidity or people who stop learning with the exception of when someone is learning a new task as then they have the patience of the Bible's Job. Said another way, 'A's appreciate competence and would prefer to spend their time with those that are continually learning and exploring what life has to offer. Keep the 'A' interested in you by having discussions on different topics and things you've read. They also love to solve problems, so bringing them problems to solve gives them purpose.

IDENTIFIABLE TALENT

'A's are incredibly observant. They don't miss much, yet rarely share all that they observe. Ironically, when a detail is missed, the 'A' can reprimand self for missing the detail forgetting that no one catches everything. They will ask self, "How did I miss that? What do I have to do differently to catch that next time?" instead of saying, "Wow, I observed over ninety percent of what was happening around me. Ya-hoo, good job." 'A's simply need to remember how incredible their observation skills are and to realize no other letter has this same ability to the same extent that they do.

IDENTIFIABLE CHALLENGE

'A's do like anything that smacks of 'you're not good enough'. Thus, their natural tendency is to shut down and quit when criticized. Instead, they must learn to breathe through the perceived insult while standing up for self. The challenge is to be able to do this without attacking the one who was criticizing.

HOW LIFE'S LESSONS APPEAR

Lessons come in three major packages: relationships; finances/resources; and health. Think about it. What lesson have you learned that did not come through one of these methodologies? The good news is that lessons that come in the other modalities are temporary inconveniences that will right themselves with time. 'A's major lessons come through relationships. Thus, if 'A's get sick, they will most often get well. Financial challenges normally disappear just as quickly as they appeared.

RELATIONSHIP OPERATIONAL STYLE

'A's can be codependent in their relationships. Webster's dictionary defines codependency as, "excessive emotional or psychological reliance on a partner". Codependency represents the ability to lose oneself in the process of being with someone else. Melody Beattie describes this type of behavior beautifully in her book, Codependent No More: How to Stop Controlling Others and Start Caring for Yourself where she explains to the naturally codependent person how to maintain healthy relationships. She does this utilizing her compassion, instructive life stories, and self-tests. The person who has a first vowel 'A' can easily be around others all day. They can enjoy their private time, yet prefer to be with people. One of the lessons in this name is to realize that we can only change ourselves and not others. Thus, it is best to work on self and not to give suggestions to others unless asked to do so.

MOTIVATION TO MAKE A PURCHASE

A's are practical. As such they don't wish to make a purchase unless they feel that it is a good deal and that the cost is reasonable for the particular product.

MOST MISCOMMUNICATIONS

The most miscommunications occur with people who have the first vowel of 'E'. This is because 'A's are more mentally oriented and 'E's are more emotionally oriented. So, one comes from the head while the other comes from the heart. Both have their advantages and disadvantages. It is helpful when 'A' remembers that it is their responsibility to learn how to speak 'E' and it is not 'E's responsibility to learn how to speak 'A'.

HOW TO INITIATE A CONVERSATION

Since 'A's love to read, ask what book they are currently reading or ask for a recommendation for a topic for which you are interested in learning more. 'A's have a wide range of interests so share interesting pieces of information that are not that well known. 'A's are hard working so anything that can effectively reduce their work load is also of interest to them. Talk to them about software that relieves them of work or other innovations that are helpful. Lastly, 'A's enjoy people so talk to them about gathering places where people discuss innovative ideas. The easiest conversation is one on books or learning.

FAVORITE IDIOM

A's often phrase their thoughts and sentences by thinking or saying, 'I think'.

.

CHAPTER THREE: FIRST VOWEL IS 'E'

"He does not preach what he practices until he has prac-
ticed what he preaches."
Confucian Project

The person whose first vowel is 'E' believes in beauty and has a sharp eye for what is attractive. The 'E's wish to look physically pleasing, even when they are slumming. This doesn't mean that 'E's are always dressed up; it does mean that they notice how an outfit looks, feels and wears. These people are usually groomed appropriately for the occasion and are constantly aware of how other people dress, not that they are judging others. Often the 'E' person will attempt to educate others on what to wear, not realizing that others may not be as concerned about appearances as they are. The 'E's feel they are helping others when giving opinions about what looks best, and how to coordinate clothing. Recipients often feel agitated and annoyed when these suggestions are uninvited. Take an 'E' shopping with you if you are one of the vowels that mainly are concerned with being comfortable, and covered, so that you'll also look great.

Due to their critical eye, the 'E' person will be the first to notice a crooked picture hanging on the wall and take action to correct the situation, often without saying a word. Thus, the 'E' will walk by the picture and gently straighten the picture out so discretely that most would not notice. The ability of having a critical eye gets expanded when 'E's decide to be helpful by letting the rest of the world know when they are failing in the decorating and beauty department. The 'E' truly believes this is a helpful characteristic and is, therefore, clueless when the recipient is not appreciative. They do not understand that the recipient may interpret their 'helpful hints' as criticism.

Touch is important to the 'E' person and they express themselves by frequently touching others to show affection. They also touch objects to become familiar with the texture. Being tactile, the 'E' persona plays with everything to know the object better and tends to mess with all of the knobs and buttons in a limousine as Tom Hanks portrayed so thoroughly in the movie "Big". This is typical behavior for the people who have the first vowel of 'E', as they literally choose to experience everything around them.

'E's learn from their feelings and are generally able to express a wide range of emotions, unless they choose the other extreme which is fear of emotion which results in suppressing their own feelings even while being able to write in a way that elicits emotions. Emotional fear expresses itself in denial, which then causes a repression of the emotion. People with the first vowel of 'E' are sensitive in the area of feelings and understand the importance of discussing them. Thus, many 'E' people are apt to ask others how they are feeling and to use sentences that start with 'I feel' unlike 'A' people who more often say 'I think'. 'E's utilize emotions to express themselves, whereas 'A's use thoughts.

In order to have clear communication with the 'E' person,

feelings must be acknowledged before the conversation can focus on other subjects. Because emotion is so important to the 'E', they often attempt to protect their feelings and become over protective of self by overeating. Thus, many 'E's will have weight challenges at some time. This can show up as being overly plump ahd/or almost anorexic in their attempt to control their desire to eat. Since the 'E' person loves beauty and food, asking them about good recipes, restaurants or cookbooks is a great way to open a conversation. Also, requesting their assistance on putting together an outfit or decorating for an event is another way to connect.

'E's would excel in the cultural setting in Mali, Africa, where the greetings are a long and important ritual that can take anywhere from five to fifteen minutes as each party asks feeling related questions of the other. The business of the day is not addressed until the proper greetings have been exchanged. This particular greeting ritual is especially hard for the 'A' person who is mentally based and wants to bypass emotions. Therefore, there is a greater chance for miscommunication between the person whose first vowel is 'A' and the person with the first vowel of 'E' than any other vowel combination. Since the 'E' person finds emotions important and is usually unable to focus on the task at hand until the emotions have been acknowledged, it is up to the 'A' person to follow this ritual and not expect the 'E' personality to adjust to the mental framework of the 'A'. All communications would benefit if everyone remembered to begin conversations with the 'E' person with a genuine question by asking how they are feeling. Interestingly, in Mali, someone's social status depends on his or her family name, not on wealth.

'E's are adept at listening to what is being said and to what is not being said. This great skill combined with their own variety of experiences allows them to offer great suggestions when people come and dump their problems on the 'E's. The hardship for the 'E' is not to accept the other person's problem and add it to their own list of problems that they are responsible for solving, making their friend's problems 'our' problems. Instead, it's important for the 'E' to be able to hand back the problem at the end of the discussion by saying, "Now that we've discussed your situation, what are you going to do about it?" The key here is the word you, as stating you, the 'E' is, in essence, handing the problem back to its original owner.

A typical 'A'-'E' miscommunication is illustrated in the story of Elle when she was driving from California to Georgia. Her friend Sarah invited her to spend the night on her trip while coming through Texas. Sarah, who made the drive to and from California and Texas frequently, informed Elle where to stop for gas, the best places along the route to eat and even where to stop for the first night to be at the midway point between their two houses, expecting her friend to arrive the second night of her trip. Sarah's 'A' shared facts to help Elle with her work of driving a long distance.

One hour away from her destination in Texas, Elle called Sarah complaining that the drive was just too long. She wanted to get a hotel room as she just could not keep driving any longer. In an effort to assist her friend, Sarah stated she would stay on the phone and talk to her friend the rest of the way. During the course of that hour, Sarah did what any good mental person would do, by repeatedly telling Elle that she could make this drive, that she was getting closer, and encouraging her to continue driving.

When Elle arrived at the house, Sarah expected a thank you for talking her friend through the situation. Instead, she was lambasted. Elle was furious. Sarah fought her urge to shut down. She was clueless and asked what the problem was. Elle explained that her feelings had been overridden and she didn't appreciate that in the least. Still confused, Sarah asked for further explanation and an example of what Elle meant. Elle complained that never once did Sarah say, "Wow, you must be really tired", or "It is really hard to drive twelve hours two days in a row", or "I understand how exhausting a long drive can be". Nothing had been said to acknowledge Elle's feelings. Sarah had mentally been encouraging Elle, yet not emotionally supporting her!

'E's seek excitement to make life less boring, as their goal is to string exciting moments together. The 'E' does not handle boredom well. They like to hear everyone's history and enjoy playing the sleuth in order to figure out what motivates others. This love of detective work makes the 'E' personality great at social gatherings, because they will interact with everyone in order to figure them out. At times, an 'E' can drain other people's energy as the 'E' is like the 'Energizer Bunny' and wants to keep partying well past when others tire. A good mystery is a favorite for the 'E' as their goal is never to have a dull moment. The detective role that Peter Falk played for years on television exemplifies these characteristics well.

Abraham Maslow defines the good life as a delicate balance between too much excitement and too little excitement. The 'E's find this a challenge as they would rather tip the scale on the side of excitement and enjoy being entertained. A good question to ask the 'E' person to start them talking is to ask what they have been doing lately for fun. The 'E's quest for excitement generates curiosity. This is often expressed as a need for freedom so that life can be fully celebrated.

This does not mean that 'E's have no quiet moments, only that they enjoy being independent rather than dominated by others. Jerry Lewis typifies the person who has 'E' for their first vowel. His ability to get emotional responses from people through his humorous movies is still classic. This talent, being able to express and feel so deeply, aided him in conveying the importance of raising money for muscular dystrophy. Jerry Lewis is well known for both his acting ability and his famous telethons.

In dealing with someone who has the first vowel of an 'E' remember:
- Ask them how they are feeling upon greeting them
- Acknowledge their feelings
- Ask their opinions on beauty
- Share personal stories with them
- Touch is important in relationships
- They have a critical eye
- As crazy as it sounds, some people do not care how they look

If you have the first vowel of an 'E', remember:
- Your job is not to educate humanity on beauty as some people are dressed for comfort only
- People who do not support you emotionally must be taught how to acknowledge your feelings, so patiently show them; it does not mean they don't care, it simply means they don't know how to support you emotionally
- Remember most people are not as empathic as you are, so tell them what you want them to know
- Remember to schedule in your playtime, you as-

sist others in remembering how to play

- Detachment is an asset, just because you are an excellent listener and give great advice to others, does not mean you have to take on their concerns making them your own.

LEARNING STYLE

There are three main learning styles, visual, auditory, and kinesthetic. The first vowel of 'E' indicates that the individual's primary way of learning is kinesthetic, with the secondary modality being auditory. Thus, when introducing the 'E' person to a new concept, it is best to provide a hands-on learning experience while talking about the subject. 'E's need to have an experience in order to learn best. Thus, informing an 'E' how to ride a bike, showing 'E' what a bike looks like, and how the gears work is totally irrelevant to having the actual experience of riding the bike. The rest of the information about the bike is superfluous until after the bike has been experienced. So, the 'E's learn by doing and having the experience.

LOVE LANGUAGE

As stated previously, each vowel shows love differently. It is important to understand how the first vowel in the name shows love so that you understand how each vowel feels love. It is wisest to show another person love in the method that they understand the best, and to receive it in the manner that you understand it best. This is similar to when two people who are native speakers in different languages wish to clearly communicate, especially if neither is fluent in the other language yet knows some of it. It is easiest to understand another when they are speaking your language, and to have the best communication, to speak to them in their native tongue. The same holds true for how we express love, our love language. If we can show love to others in the style that they can easily recognize then we are doing a better job of communicating our feelings.

So, 'E's typically show their love for you by telling you in a romantic way such as writing their love for you in a poem or using flowery language. They can be seductive in their actions by writing you love poems, by surprising you with flowers or by buying you candy, lighting candles, and/or wearing intimate, enticing clothing. 'E's are most appreciative and recognize that you are saying, "I love you" when you take your time to get a bit mushy, and to touch them. Also, recognize that they are saying to you that you are loved when they touch you and create a romantic environment.

If you are in love with a person who has a first vowel of 'E', touch them as you walk by them; put your hand on their shoulders or arm when in public and be ready for a bit of cuddling and affection. 'E's love touch and the feel of things, so wear something soft and either a bit tight, or it has a low neckline, or if male, no shirt, or somehow enhance the physical aspects of your body. Making love is the quintessential way of showing 'E's they are loved since they identify touch with being loved. 'E's find it challenging to follow the guideline of no PDA (public displays of affection).

COMMUNICATION STYLE

'E's start conversations with, "How are you?" because they genuinely care how you are. They chit chat about the happenings of the previous day and what occurred earlier in the same day. They automatically connect with other people as they are naturally people oriented. 'E's can often feel as if 'A's don't care about them because 'A's tend to focus on work prior to any type of socializing. This disturbs the 'E' as the 'E's understand that connecting with people is far more important than getting work done. 'E's don't need to be in charge unless one of the following combinations occur, 'KE', 'CE' or 'EL' at the start of the name. When these combinations start the name, the individual tends to be a highly conscious leader who inspires others as they have both the mental frame of mind to be a great leader and compassion. Thus, everyone benefits when 'KE', 'CE', or 'EL' lead.

GIFT PREFERENCES

Gift shopping for the person whose first vowel is 'E' is relatively easy because they love anything of beauty or that brings excitement or adventure into their lives, like a ticket to a play. They also enjoy items that help them to feel good, such as beauty products, new clothes, a massage, sensory bath products or art.

'E's love beauty and magic so anything, within their taste, that enhances their surroundings is appreciated. Since the 'E' is tactile, they will appreciate experiences, or a day at the spa. They would also enjoy bath products, perfume, or cologne that would enhance their tactile experiences. Since

'E's notice how things look and how things feel, they appreciate gifts that are soft to the touch and that are beautiful, besides those gifts that smell good. They appreciate spa days, massages, or possibly getting their nails or hair done. They enjoy good clothes, and beautiful objects to use to decorate the house. Taking the 'E' out to a fancy restaurant where the food is exquisite and smells great is also a treat. An incredible treat would be hiring a cleaning crew to clean every nook and cranny of the house, from the top of the ceiling fans to underneath the beds. Your 'E' will notice how clean the house is and will gratefully appreciate it.

HOW TO MAINTAIN A LONG RELATION-SHIP

'E's appreciate great communication and touch. Hugs are important as they convey that you care for the 'E'. 'E's like to be told that they are important to you and that you appreciate them. They need to feel needed and enjoy time with friends and family, even if it's spent just watching television together. Often you'll find that the 'E' has fix-it-up projects and enjoys having company during the process. Keeping your friend that has the first vowel of 'E' company and keeping in touch lets the 'E' know you care and keeps the relationship going forward.

IDENTIFIABLE TALENT

'E's are great listeners and great detectives. They hear what is said and what is not said as they have the ability to almost feel what another person is going through. They will get to know people a lot faster than most as people feel so comfortable telling the 'E' their deepest secrets. 'E's are talented problem solvers as they use their investigation skills to figure out the various parts of the puzzle, be it personal, technical, or managerial, to find a viable solution.

IDENTIFIABLE CHALLENGE

A challenge that 'E's face is to become too emotionally involved in other people's problems by treating the problem as if it is their responsibility to solve, as if it was originally their problem. They can become too emotional over small incidences or when things do not go their way. Two great books for the 'E's to digest are; Emotional Literacy by Claude Steiner and The Emotion Code by Dr. Bradley Nelson. Both books excel at educating individuals on how to raise their emotional IQs so that they can achieve better personal and professional relationships.

HOW LIFE'S LESSONS APPEAR

Lessons come in three major packages: relationships; finances/resources; and health. Think about it. What lesson have you learned that did not come through one of these methodologies? The good news is that whatever method is used to receive lessons, the other modalities are normally only temporary problems, not permanent ones. So, lessons that come in the other modalities are temporary inconveniences that will right themselves with time. 'E's major lessons come through health.

RELATIONSHIP OPERATIONAL STYLE

'E's usually are passive-aggressive in their relationships. Webster's dictionary defines passive-aggressive as "indirect resistance to the demands of others and an avoidance of direct confrontation, as in procrastinating, pouting, or misplacing important materials." 'E's are normally sensitive to other emotions; thus, 'E's can resort to the passive-aggressive approach in an attempt to avoid hurting another's feelings. They simply do not realize that being passive-aggressive, is in itself, is hurtful. Linda Siegmund's book, <u>In Sheep's Clothing: Understanding and Dealing with Manipulative People</u> illustrates how other's feel when they are manipulated by passive-aggressive behaviors, and what can be done to improve these situations.

MOTIVATION TO MAKE A PURCHASE

'E's are motivated to make a purchase after they bond with the salesperson on an emotional level. Since 'E's are aesthetic, they want to touch and/or feel the product prior to purchasing. Know that how something looks, feels, and smells will be important to the 'E' buyer.

MOST MISCOMMUNICATIONS

The most miscommunications occur with people who have the first vowel of 'A'. This is because 'A's are more mentally oriented, so the orientation is from the mind. 'E's are more emotionally oriented, so the orientation is from the heart. These approaches are opposite from each other in both conception and delivery. Both have their advantages and disadvantages. It is helpful when 'E' remembers to teach 'A's how best to talk with them.

HOW TO INITIATE A CONVERSATION

'E's enjoy solving the problems that keep others up at night in the area of personal relationships. They also love to laugh. So, approach an 'E' either seeking advice or with a request for a story. You can also simply say, "Heard any good news today?". The 'E' will take this clue and share something amazing or funny that happened in their day. 'E's are the easiest of all of the vowels for most people to converse. Why? Because they know how to listen and hear what is being said as well as what is not being said. They can see both the big picture of the problem being presented and the details that went astray. Best yet, they can come up with a viable solution to a wide variety of problems. It is in everyone's best interest to have an 'E' as a confidant in their lives.

FAVORITE IDIOM

'E's often phrase their thoughts and sentences by thinking or saying, "I feel".

CHAPTER FOUR: FIRST VOWEL IS 'I'

"You can only get love from other people if you first love yourself."

Shawn Rae, Global Goodwill Ambassador for the World Energy Forum

Family issues dominate people who have 'I' as the first vowel, which can be positive or negative in nature. On the positive side, family is critical to the 'I', and often the 'I' feels responsible for his or her parents especially as the parents' age. The 'I' person can feel that s/he is responsible for other family members as well and that it may be necessary to play the mediator. On the negative side, issues with family may include unresolved feelings of abandonment or ill treatment in childhood, like not getting enough attention while a child. Some 'I' children have learned to create scenes in school merely to gain the attention that they crave from home. Other 'I's have used their issues to propel them forward as Sigmund Freud did.

The 'I' person is emotionally involved with his or her own family. Therefore, it is highly important that the family unit looks cohesive and trouble free to the public. A child of 'I' parents usually feels one extreme or the other; parents are overly involved in their lives or they are being ignored. 'I' people learn from family, while they are being kept busy helping other relatives or dealing with their own issues that stem from childhood. If unsatisfied with their childhood, the 'I's readily put blame on how they were treated by their parents regardless if their parents deserved to be criticized.

A person who typifies the need for a coherent family, yet consistently had family issues was past President Bill Clinton. Remember how many times he made the news for his extramarital affairs with Monica Lewinsky and Paula Jones, and how important it was for his wife Hillary to publicly support him? Now Hillary's name also has the first vowel of 'I', so the appearance of a cohesive perfect family would be important to her also.

Due to being overly influenced by family, 'I's become survivors. They learn to last through any situation and are action oriented. Once a dear friendship is made with a person whose first vowel is 'I', the friend is considered and treated as family.

The "I' symbolizes somewhat of a paradox in that it represents either 'I am first' or 'my family is first'. Hence the 'I' person takes care of self primarily so that s/he can take care of others. This is not a selfish position in the eyes of the 'I' as how can one take care of family if not able to take care of self? Nikola Tesla, one of the most brilliant scientists to date, demonstrated this by taking such extreme, precautionary care of self, so he could live long enough to demonstrate how it is possible to provide free electricity to the world, thus taking care of others. Often times the 'I' is labeled an idealist. The easiest way to connect with an 'I' is to inquire about his/her family. On rare occasions, you'll find an 'I' who has abandoned his/her family in order to gain some sense of peace. This is against what they are here to learn and is troublesome. When this occurs, quickly reword your question about family to asking them what they would consider the perfect family.

The 'I' persona needs to feel included. This characteristic makes a wondrous motivational point when wanting to teach something to 'I's, as 'I's do not like to be out of the loop. People with the first vowel of 'I' get physically sick when they do not receive enough attention from others. Therefore, when disciplining a child whose first vowel is 'I', simply state that it is easier for others to include them when the disagreeable behavior is not present. Another successful method is to give them a time-out, hence removing them from others, until the unwanted behavior is under control. Since it is important for the 'I' to feel included, they will often poke into other people's personal business to satisfy this need.

The 'I' personality enjoys being the focal point or in a leadership role and is a natural leader. In other words, whether appointed to lead or not, others perceive the 'I' person is in charge. Coworkers find the 'I' personality easy to approach when asking questions. Most of the time the 'I' persona has the answer as the 'I' dislikes not being in the know. A challenge for the 'I' personality is, when clueless, not to create an imaginative answer when peers ask for assistance. Again, an excellent example of these characteristics is Bill Clinton. During his presidency, he was a natural leader, optimistic and easily approachable. He also exhibited the 'I' characteristic of making up an answer when at a loss, as when he created the new definition for the word sex. A creed 'I's use is: "If I can't dazzle them with brilliance, I'll baffle them with bullshit."

'I's prefer harmony and work hard at maintaining a sense

of serenity. They don't handle anger well. Peacefulness with others in the workplace is easiest for 'I's with people whose first vowels are 'A', 'E', 'U' or 'Y'. However, they feel challenged with people who have the first vowel of either 'I' or 'O' as competition is aroused. 'I' personalities need to feel that they are competent at their jobs, even on the rare occasions when they are not. 'I's take their role as leaders seriously; it is what gives them purpose and value.

The more 'I's in a name, the more the person has a tendency to be 'me first' oriented, self-absorbed or self-centered. While the focus is on the first vowel, it is important to remember that the placement of the 'I' in the name determines the meaning. Only when the first vowel is 'I' does the letter carry the family issue to the extent discussed here.

In dealing with someone who has the first vowel of an 'I' remember:
- They are natural leaders
- Family comes first
- They need to be included and kept informed
- Buy them gifts they have stated are wanted
- Give them attention
- They are survivors and will outlast you
- They give great advice
- They are idealistic
- It does not mean you are disliked if you were not included

If you have the first vowel of an 'I', remember:
- You don't really have to know everything other people know
- It's okay for the family to have problems, as they

are your best teachers
- It is not your job to rescue other members of your family
- It is okay to go beyond the limitations of your parents
- You are not alone
- Any gift given means you were thought of, just because others did not remember your hints does not mean you are not loved

LEARNING STYLE

There are three main learning styles, visual, auditory, and kinesthetic. The first vowel of 'I' indicates that the individual's primary way of learning is auditory, with the secondary modality being kinesthetic. Thus, when introducing the 'I' person to a new concept, it is best to talk about the subject and secondly to give the person a hands-on learning experience. 'I's need to have be able to repeatedly hear something new in order to learn best. So, recording the lessons and replaying that tape continuously is the best. So, the 'I's learn by hearing the material that is being presented and secondarily having the experience.

LOVE LANGUAGE

As stated previously, each vowel shows love differently. It is important to understand how the first vowel in the name shows love so that you understand how each vowel feels love. It is wisest to show another person love in the method that they understand the best, and to receive it in the manner that you understand it best. This is similar to when two people who are native speakers in different languages wish to clearly communicate, especially if neither is fluent in the other language yet knows some of it. It is easiest to understand another when they are speaking your language, and to have the best communication, to speak to them in their native tongue. The same holds true for how we express love, our love language. If we can show love to others in the style that they can easily recognize then we are doing a better job of communicating our feelings.

So, 'I's typically show their love for you by including you in what they are doing. 'I's will take you with them on their trips and include you in as many of their activities as they possibly can. They also love to be included in your activities. This is the one vowel that could be with their loved one twenty-four hours a day and enjoy every minute of it. 'I's feel loved when they know they are wanted. Anything that is said or done which implies inclusivity is how love, for an 'I', is both felt and expressed.

COMMUNICATION STYLE

'I's start conversations with something that is happening in their lives or the lives of their families. They love to be included, so if not wishing to talk about family affairs, ask if the 'I' would like to join you and your friends the next time you get together. Being included is crucial and so immediately including the 'I' in your activities is the way to bond with the 'I'.

GIFT PREFERENCES

Remember that the 'I' person needs attention. Hence, they drop hints about what they want for a gift. They expect people. who really care for them to pick up on these hints and buy accordingly. Another idea is to purchase something that would improve their life by saving them time or making something easier. Either of these ideas will work. However, if a hint has not been dropped nor an item to simplify their life observed, then simply ask them what is wanted. Asking is preferred over purchasing a gift that will not be valued, as 'I's know what they want. 'I's are actually the easiest people to purchase gifts for if you simply ask them for their list. They inevitably have a list of desired items. Ask what color, size, and/or other specifics would naturally go with the item on their list that you intend to purchase for them. Get them exactly an item from their list to their specifications, and they will love the gift.

'I's are not interested in how much a gift cost. They are interested in knowing that you cared enough to ask them what they wanted and actually purchased it for them. Shopping for the 'I' person can take extra effort and planning as the gift must say that you were listening to them and did a great deal of thinking on their behalf. The gift has to be something that the 'I' person had stated is wanted or a gift that you noticed he or she could use to make his or her life easier. The recipient of the gift is easily insulted if the foregoing conditions are not been met as the 'I' feels you are giving them a gift out of obligation and not from truly caring.

HOW TO MAINTAIN A LONG RELATIONSHIP

It is important to 'I's to be included, so if you wish to maintain a long-term relationship with 'I's invite them to your house to holiday events and meet them frequently for lunch or other activities. Call the 'I' on a fairly regular basis as it shows that you care. Remember their birthdays and special holidays with notes and/or gifts. Being thought of and included is so important to 'I's. Including them in your life on a regular basis is what keeps this friendship going strong.

IDENTIFIABLE TALENT

'I's are natural leaders. Regardless of who is assigned to be the leader, people will gravitate toward the 'I' and ask the 'I' what most would have thought the boss was better able to answer. It is simply easy to talk with the 'I' and easier for people not to feel that they will be in trouble for not knowing something. 'I's are great working independently and giving suggestions to others on how to solve life's problems. They just seem to know how things ought to work. They are naturally great leaders.

IDENTIFIABLE CHALLENGE

A challenge faced by the 'I's is knowing when to step aside and when to be the leader. The 'I's are natural leaders and yet, at times, not so great at following. They tend to forget that the best leaders were first the best followers. Imagine a general in the service; that person had to first be a great soldier who followed orders. Each step of the way, each advancement, the person had to prove self in each successive position until he became the best leader because he worked under and observed other leaders and learned from them. So, the challenge is to learn as much as possible from each person with which they work whereby they can be the best leader possible when it is their turn to lead. A great book to read on leadership is Extreme Ownership: How U.S. Navy SEALS Lead and Win by Jacko Willink and Leif Babin who learned extremely valuable lessons through success and failure. They learned from their errors what worked and what did not. Constantly refining their efforts led them to develop a highly effective methodology that is easy to copy for leaders in all sorts of positions. So, natural leaders can refine their talents by adding to their natural gifts by implementing the principles that they executed.

HOW LIFE'S LESSONS APPEAR

Lessons come in three major packages: relationships; finances/resources; and health. Think about it. What lesson have you learned that did not come through one of these methodologies? The good news is that whatever method is used to receive lessons, the other modalities are normally only temporary problems, not permanent ones. So, lessons that come in the other modalities are temporary inconveniences that will right themselves with time. 'I's major lessons come through relationships and mostly family relationships and those individuals that feel like family.

RELATIONSHIP OPERATIONAL STYLE

'I's are usually interdependent in their relationships. Webster's dictionary defines interdependency as "the dependence of two or more people on each other." They wish for connectivity and at the same time 'I's wish for independence. This can be a challenging balance to maintain. Thus, in every day they desire to have both alone time and together time. They do not appreciate being smothered nor do they wish to be with others twenty-four hours a day. This has nothing to do with their partner, friends, or family. Instead, it has to do with their wish to have time alone to create, to think, and to reflect on their thoughts and the thoughts of others. Interdependent relationships work. A great book on how to achieve a close relationship utilizing this methodology is Interdependent Minds: The dynamics of Close Relationships by Sandra Murray and John Holmes. Interdependent relationships normally work well.

MOTIVATION TO MAKE A PURCHASE

Since I's learn their lessons via relationships and major in family relationships, most 'I's consider their family when making a large purchase. For example, is the back seat of the car comfortable enough for the entire family? Is this a movie the entire family would enjoy? Is this a house that has enough room for the entire family to have their own space? Purchases are made when the purchase benefits the entire household in some manner.

MOST MISCOMMUNICATIONS

Due to 'I's being natural leaders they can have the most miscommunications with the first vowel of 'O' since the 'O's are the assigned leaders. 'I's and 'O's may not always see eye-to-eye on what the appropriate way is to lead, and hence the misunderstanding can occur. Also, when the 'I's listen to the boss it's important that they really hear what the boss has to say and not what they wish the boss had said. This is because others are going to ask the 'I' what was said when they forget and that is when the 'I' is going to say what they thought they heard. This is another opportunity for a misunderstanding. The 'I's need to be sure only to answer what they know to be true and not to make up the difference for what they think may be true.

HOW TO INITIATE A CONVERSATION

The I's are the easiest to start a conversation; all one needs to do is ask if they have kids or some other question about the family. 'I's can talk what seems like forever once they get on the topic of their family. Other than suggesting your family and theirs would love to get together, keep your family out of the conversation. Simply be in awe of theirs.

FAVORITE IDIOM

'I's often phrase their thoughts and sentences by thinking or saying. "I see".

41

CHAPTER FIVE: FIRST VOWEL IS 'O'

"While we learn from pain, we heal through love"
Stephanie Austin

People who have the first vowel of 'O' need to be the boss, whether it is in charge of a family, in control of a classroom, the head of the project or preferably the CEO of the entire company. The 'O' person feels insulted to be micromanaged as the 'O' works best independently and does not tolerate someone looking too closely over his or her shoulder or attempting to control him/her by giving orders. Of course, the 'O' will get the job done and get it done well. The best approach with a person whose first vowel is 'O' is to remember that the 'O' wants to be asked, not told, what to do. Coupled with this characteristic, 'O's do not like to be asked twice. They remember hearing it the first time and will decide for themselves what is important and when to get it done. They definitely hate being nagged, and a simple reminder to them feels like nagging.

Paradoxically, the 'O' personality needs to feel useful at all times, and therefore, complies with most requests. News anchorman Tom Brokaw exemplifies the characteristics of 'O' in how he gives the impression that he is taking care of business. No matter how bad the news is, somehow we are going to make it come out okay. It is as though Brokaw were a mother lion protecting his crew of cubs. Another media personality that is a great example of the first vowel 'O' protecting her cubs is Oprah Winfrey. Both of these well-known television personalities combine their being useful with nurturing the ones around them.

The 'O's are natural nurturers and thus desire to be protective of other people with whom they feel close. They often feel this is a thankless position much like the 'A' personality when they feel unappreciated. The 'O' persona will nurture those around them even when others do not care to be nurtured. To satisfy this ingrained need, 'O's usually have pets. When meeting the 'O' for the first time and wanting to start a conversation, simply ask if the 'O' has a beloved animal at home.

'O's generally have magnetic personalities. Think Tom Cruise. People are naturally drawn to 'O's. However, like the 'E' personality, if they are not happy they can ruin the party for everybody. Remember when Tom Cruise badmouthed Brooke Shields because she decided to get help for her postpartum depression. Since Tom thinks it is wrong, it is wrong for everyone.

The 'O' can be moody when feeling insignificant. They can also be quite controlling, yet would not think of self as such since they are simply taking care of the job and have others best interest in mind. When in charge, the 'O' boss wants things done his/her way.

The 'O' persona carries volumes of responsibility well; however, on the rare occasion when the 'O' becomes overwhelmed, he/she projects his/her own faults onto others. Again, think of Tom Cruise and his demeanor on the Today Show where he revisited the question of psychiatry and medication. His position was that others were ill informed about the role of psychiatry, not considering that, perhaps, he too did not have all of the answers.

The 'O' personality requires loyalty from others and feels this is the least that can be expected because others have benefited from the 'O's natural nurturing characteristics and the ability of the 'O' to keep their best interests in mind. Therefore, the 'O' feels others should be beholden to them. Thus, 'O's carry a grudge when they feel they have been wronged. It is wise never to betray the 'O' as it will be hard for them to forgive or forget. Now think about Brooke Shields who handled the above incident with Tom Cruise gracefully. She benefited from her double 'OO' as her ability to love and nurture were enhanced.

Lastly, 'O's prefer a fairly regular routine. It is not that they are nonflexible as others would accuse them of being; it is simply because they find life more satisfying when they follow a routine. Besides, having a routine helps them cram all that they schedule into a single day and enables them to get it all done. 'O's are some of the few people who genuinely multitask well.

In dealing with someone who has the first vowel of an 'O' remember:
- They have to be the boss of something
- They don't want someone watching over their shoulder too closely
- They have a great sense of fair play
- They are the natural nurturers
- When upset, they project their faults onto others
- They need to feel useful

- They have magnetic personalities
- Other people are competent too

If you have the first vowel of an 'O', remember:
- Not everyone needs nurturing
- Others may not interpret your sense of fairness as fair
- People do not doubt you when they ask why you made a particular decision; they want to learn from you
- It's okay just to be the boss of yourself
- Your friends/family may not be able to afford the expensive gift you crave so generosity is not to be equated with how much a person loves you

LEARNING STYLE

There are three main learning styles, visual, auditory and kinesthetic. The first vowel of 'O' indicates that the individual's primary way of learning is visual, with the secondary modality being kinesthetic. Like the 'A', when introducing the 'O' person to a new concept, it is best to provide a visual picture of the concept, and/or a one -page summary for the 'O' to read later. Remember, they are practical and if given too much material, they will think it's crazy to have to read that much when it can be condensed, so provide a brief summary. Being visual, the 'O' will take copious notes when interested in a subject as it helps their memory when they can refer to the notes later. Notes are not hand written, but typed on a computer, since many 'O's are pressed for time and thus their handwriting can be a challenge to read later. 'O's generally tend to learn concepts in depth, and naturally have great test taking abilities. 'O's recall is amazing once a subject has been studied.

LOVE LANGUAGE

Each vowel shows love differently. It is important to understand how the first vowel in the name shows love so that you understand how each vowel feels love. How one shows love is saying how one perceives they are loved. It is wisest to show another person love in the method that they understand the best, and to receive it in the manner that you understand it best. This is similar to when two people who are native speakers in different languages wish to clearly communicate, especially if neither is fluent in the other person's language, yet knows some the language. The clearest communication takes place when one hears their native tongue and then speaks the other one's native language back to them. The same holds true for how we express love, our love language. If we can show love to others in the style that they can easily recognize then we are doing a better job of communicating our feelings.

Like the 'E's, 'O's can be quite physically affectionate in their relationships. So, expect lots of physical contact in a loving way. They too have a challenge in abiding by society's no PDF (public display of affection) rule. Consistent with their love of money, if they share their earnings with you, then they are showing you that they care, and you are loved. Conversely, they feel loved when both affection and finances are shared with them.

COMMUNICATION STYLE

The 'O's are very direct and say what they mean. They may or may not utilize tact. They can be incredibly loving and/or so blunt that one is taken aback. They don't mince words. You will always know where you stand when you are with an 'O'. There shall be no doubt in your mind if they don't care for something you have done as they will vocalize it immediately. 'O's can be incredibly sweet and romantic with their words and also incredibly harsh. The only concern for others is when the 'O' gets a bit bossy because no adult enjoys being told what to do; they'd rather be asked. Be sure you don't nag the 'O' as that is their pet peeve and wakes the dragon in them.

GIFT PREFERENCES

The other letter that knows what they want is the 'O' and they usually announce it ahead of time. Frequently they remind others that their birthday is approaching. The 'O' expects something expensive to show them how much you care while reemphasizing that they are important and the boss. When shopping for someone whose first vowel is 'O', buy something expensive as they often judge how much they are loved by how much you spent on them. There are no exceptions to this, even as the 'O' will deny this is true as they don't want other people to know how much value they place on money. Easier yet, simply write them a check or give them money. The larger the amount, the better. Then the 'O' can combine your gift with other money gifts and buy themselves the expensive item that they really wanted.

HOW TO MAINTAIN A LONG RELATIONSHIP

To maintain a long-time relationship with 'O's ,a person needs to know how to take directions and not have to be the leader. Make suggestions and use tact as the 'O's are not amenable to being told what to do nor to being nagged. 'O's are affectionate and nurturing, so give just as much as you receive. They are quite thoughtful and require their friends to be appreciative of all of the little things that the 'O' does on their behalf. Staying grateful, being generous, and willing to constantly have new adventures together is what keeps 'O's in their relationships.

IDENTIFIABLE TALENT

'O's can juggle more items and keep them straight more than any other letters plus they nurture others while doing so. 'O's know how to love others and really open their hearts up. You know it when an 'O' loves you!

IDENTIFIABLE CHALLENGE

'O's can become bossy when not getting their own way. This is a turn off to everyone else in the relationship. When not getting what they want the 'O' would benefit from talking it out and getting clarity from the other person and then duplicating the mediation skills of the 'A'.

HOW LIFE'S LESSONS APPEAR

Lessons come in three major packages: relationships; finances/resources; and health. Think about it. What lesson have you learned that did not come through one of these methodologies? The good news is that whatever method is used to receive lessons, the other modalities are normally only temporary problems, not permanent ones. So, lessons that come in the other modalities are temporary inconveniences that will right themselves with time. 'O's major lessons come through finances and how they use their resources.

RELATIONSHIP OPERATIONAL STYLE

'O's can be domineering in their relationships. Webster's dictionary defines domineering as, "assert one's will over another in an arrogant way". This is because 'O's are either the boss or have autonomy in their work place and carry that over into their other relationships where they think they are still the boss. There is a great book, Recovering Confidence: A Guide for Male Survivors of Domineering Women by Thorn Wright. Even though the title indicates that the book is written for males, women who have had men dominate them can learn from this book also. One has to rebuild confidence once one has slowly been beaten down in order to recover and heal so that they can create appropriate relationships in the future.

MOTIVATION TO MAKE A PURCHASE

O's love to tell others what to do. Thus, 'O's are motivated to purchase quality, expensive items, many of a technical nature, from someone who knows how to take direction from them and give great service.

MOST MISCOMMUNICATIONS

Due to 'I's being natural leaders they can have the most miscommunications with the first vowel of 'O' since the 'O's are the assigned leaders. 'I's and 'O's may not always see eye-to-eye on what the appropriate way is to lead, and hence the misunderstanding can occur. The 'O' expects their leadership to be followed and finds it difficult when challenged by 'I's. Thus, there is more opportunity for miscommunication as both the 'O' and 'I' wish to lead. It is the 'O's position to be the leader and the 'I's to be the follower in this regard.

HOW TO INITIATE A CONVERSATION

'O's can talk about work, both problems and solutions all day long. They can also speak to any of their hobbies and most have pets and are willing to talk about them just as much as they can talk about work. Start by asking if the 'O' has a pet and then use follow-up questions from there. Thus, it behooves one to address an 'O' by either a pet conversation or a work conversation.

FAVORITE IDIOM

'O's often phrase their thoughts and sentences by thinking or saying, "I know".

CHAPTER SIX: FIRST VOWEL IS 'U'

"I appreciate your brain, you use your right brain, your left brain, and your hair brain."
    Shawn Rae, Global Goodwill Ambassador for the World
    Energy Forum

People who have the first vowel of a 'U' are interesting when they talk. They are the entertainers and storytellers which is why so many of the more popular artists have this for their first vowel: Lucille Ball, Hugh Grant, Russell Crowe, Julianne Hough 45 , Julianne Moore, Julia Styles, Julia Roberts, and Jude Law. They are the communicators. When relating a story or idea, they are animated and enthusiastic. These people are known to melt hearts when they flash one of their genuine smiles; visualize Julia Robert's smile. The 'U' encourages others to lighten up so that everyone can get more enjoyment from life on a daily basis.

People with the first vowel of 'U' ideally add adventure to each of their days. This letter represents humor, laughter and affection personified except when tamed by other, more grounded letters in their name like 'B', 'C', 'K', 'M', 'N' or 'S'. When there is a more grounded letter next to the 'U', it means the person is serious at work yet playful elsewhere.

'U's need to feel they are effective in their endeavors.

The 'U's personality is similar to the chameleon, as they will adapt themselves to fit any crowd to gain the attention they desire as well as exhibiting traits of all the other vowels. They see themselves in everyone else. This quality has greatly helped Insytle Inc founder Sister June Canoles when teaching others how to analyze handwriting as her students learn through humor coupled with her understanding of their personality traits as evidenced in their handwriting.

In the midst of capturing an audience with a story, the 'U' will tend to exaggerate parts of the tale in order to keep the audience enthralled. Hence the tendency to blur fantasy and reality has the 'U' appearing dishonest at times. This same trait represents a fine line separating the real from the unreal, thus making spirituality or religion plausible for the 'U' as they find surreal facts totally believable. Some would say activist and radio personality Rush Limbaugh is a good example of one who epitomizes this trait with his Republican voice that people either love or hate. Other letters in his name say he is honestly dedicated to wanting freedom for all individuals.

The big picture is easy to see for a 'U'; however, seeing all the details can be a challenge. Thinking outside of the box is normal yet, the 'U' often lacks attention to details unless other letters (like 'S' or 'N') in the name carry the detail aspect. When working on a project, a nice balance is created when a 'U' person is paired with the detailed oriented 'A' or 'O' person.

'U's have an incredibly short attention span when the topic is boring. Due to the need to be entertained and to avoid boredom, the 'U' can appear impatient or needing to be the center of attention. In reality, the 'U' is so concerned for others that they are overprotective of their loved ones, and hence, can drain energy from others when they are meaning to give it. People with the first vowel of 'U' definitely live in the moment. Since the 'U' rarely holds someone's past against them, they are able to give great advice.

The 'U' persona also does what he or she thinks is best in the long run for the people with whom he or she interacts; as such, 'U's feel they are sharing unconditionally. Recipients often interpret this behavior as being judgmental. The misconception occurs over the understanding of the definition of unconditional love. The recipient often believes unconditional love means being completely accepted, and the 'U' feels unconditional love means doing what is right and best for others even when it is unpopular. Susan Sarandon falls into this category in the movie The Banger Sisters. The 'U' sees this as self-sacrificing. In sharing this version of love, the 'U' feels similar to people that have the first vowel of 'A'; they have given for the good of others even though those on the receiving end would disagree. Whereas it is rarely noticed when 'A' donates time and energy for the good of others, the 'U' self-sacrifices in a way that is noticed, is frequently misinterpreted, and therefore not appreciated by others. When 'U' is the first vowel in the name, you have people who are superb entertainers and know how to party.

In dealing with someone who has the first vowel of 'U' remember:
- They have short attention spans
- They give great advice
- They have a great sense of play and humor
- They tend to exaggerate
- They are the entertainers

- Whatever you share could become their next story

If you have the first vowel of an 'U', remember:
- As great as your tales are, people appreciate you not embellishing a story
- It's okay to have times when you are not "on"
- You are easily liked just the way you are, so you don't have to prove anything to anyone
- Quiet time is not your enemy
- You don't have to please every single person
- Stories are great on their own merit without embellishment

LEARNING STYLE

There are three main learning styles, visual, auditory, and kinesthetic. The first vowel of 'U' indicates that the individual's primary way of learning is kinesthetic, with the secondary modality being visual. Thus, both 'E' and 'U's main methodology is kinesthetic, yet their secondary methodologies are different. Same as the 'E', when introducing the 'U' person to a new concept, it is best to provide a hands-on learning experience while talking about the subject. 'E's need to have an experience in order to learn best. Thus, teaching 'U' how to ride a bike, showing 'U' what a bike looks like, and how the gears work is totally irrelevant to having the actual experience of riding the bike. The rest of the information about the bike is superfluous until after the bike has been experienced. So, the 'U's learn by doing and having the experience.

LOVE LANGUAGE

Each vowel shows love differently. It is important to understand how the first vowel in the name shows love so that you understand how each vowel feels love. How one shows love is saying how one perceives they are loved. It is wisest to show another person love in the method that they understand the best, and to receive it in the manner that you understand it best. This is similar to when two people who are native speakers in different languages wish to clearly communicate, especially if neither is fluent in the other person's language, yet knows some the language. The clearest communication takes place when one hears their native tongue and then speaks the other one's native language back to them. The same holds true for how we express love, our love language. If we can show love to others in the style that they can easily recognize then we are doing a better job of communicating our feelings.

The 'U' is an easy letter to love as these people love to have fun. Fun can be defined as anything that brings them pleasure, that keeps them amused, or that is simply a great diversion from the tasks at hand. Playfulness, teasing, and surprising them with unexpected treats are all ways that the 'U' understands they are loved. 'U's can handle seriousness, but not for an extended period of time. So, keeping the relationship light, showing them fun, and listening to their stories lets the 'U' feel loved.

Security is also important to the 'U', so providing adequate finances so they don't have to be concerned on how things shall be paid, is a real winner for the 'U'. In other words, treating the 'U' and paying for your outings lets the 'U' know that they are loved.

COMMUNICATIONS

The 'U's expect you to read their minds and often speak around their feelings until they have stewed on their feelings for such a long time that they want to blow up instead of talking it out while the issue is still small. They can blow things out of proportion due to their love of drama. The 'U' will often deny that their life is full of drama, yet if you look at how they live their life actual is, it'll be apparent that it is full of crisis created by the 'U' and the ones around them. Often 'U's will have the best boundaries of any vowel except for the 'O's; the difference is that they express their boundaries in a very loving and extremely clear way. 'U's will discuss the same emotional topic repeatedly until they final clear it which may be way past your tolerance level for listening to the same problem repeatedly. Friends of 'U's need to be equally as clear with their boundaries for the friendships to really work. That way mutual respect is established. 'U's are extremely loyal to their friends. An intimate friendship takes longer to establish as most of the time people are kept as acquaintances because it's easier to have fun that way and to make sure the relationship doesn't get too serious.

GIFT PREFERENCES

Shopping for 'U's is easy as they enjoy gifts that remind them of fun or anything that creates an opportunity to play. Buy them an experience that they would not have had otherwise: a theater ticket, a train ride, a fancy meal, a cultural experience or even a toy to emphasis their playfulness. A gift certificate is also wondrous for a 'U' because these people love to window shop, and it gives them an excuse to buy.

The 'U' is the entertainer; they appreciate gifts that entertain like tickets to plays, a game or a decorative piece. 'U's also love receiving money because it provides the means for them to entertain themselves while window shopping and using their imagination considering what they can buy with this money. In contrast, the practical 'A' would spend the money paying bills, and the 'O' would pay off his or her credit card with the money as they purchased something expensive. The 'I' would be insulted that the gift giver had not taken the time to listen and get what they had hinted they wanted, and the 'Y' would consider the person lazy as they could have earned the money themselves. Actually, what the 'U' wants most is your company! So, take the 'U' out to a fancy restaurant where they haven't dined previously, or to the theater, or ice-skating. Simply be with them and make it fun.

HOW TO MAINTAIN A LONG RELATIONSHIP

'U's have a short attention span. So, keep them guessing what you are going to do next yet be true to your word and follow through on promises. The 'U' needs to be able to depend on you, so don't say you are going to do something without actually following through. 'U's like to have regular connections. The preference is for daily contact, but at the bare minimum, they expect to connect once a week. Time together can be short or long; it simply needs to happen. It doesn't matter if the connection is in person or on the phone. Simply the connection needs to be there. 'U's can be driven a bit crazy when there are inconsistent communications. So, stay in touch. This is a friendship that is either worth your time or not, but it will definitely take time to keep going. Do realize that 'U's will always be there for you if you need assistance. You simply need to be able to keep up the consistent contact with them.

IDENTIFIABLE TALENT

'U's can see the big picture when creating something new. They excel at being original and love to share imaginative ideas. They are ingenuous, being both inventive and resourceful. One could even consider them clever to some extent.

IDENTIFIABLE CHALLENGE

With such an incredible imagination it's easy to see that 'U's can overly exaggerate or fabricate their stories. You will be entertained, however, you may wish to double check facts prior to acting on what the 'U' has shared since their ability to prevaricate is quite astonishing. Now, do they all do this? At times they do, but it is inconsistent because sometimes they are not exaggerating what has actually happened. Hence, engage your discerning ears when listening to the 'U'.

HOW LIFE'S LESSONS APPEAR

Lessons come in three major packages: relationships; finances/resources; and health. Think about it. What lesson have you learned that did not come through one of these methodologies? The good news is that whatever method is used to receive lessons, the other modalities are normally only temporary problems, not permanent ones. So, lessons that come in the other modalities are temporary inconveniences that will right themselves with time. 'U's major lessons come through health. It is advisable for the 'U's to jump on any illness immediately as they are most susceptible to contracting life-long ailments that slowly drain them of their ability to get a good night's sleep and/or have enough energy to get through the day. Thus, it's important to attend to one's health issues immediately.

RELATIONSHIP OPERATIONAL STYLE

U's usually are both indirect and direct vocally in their relationships. Webster's dictionary defines direct as "extending" or "moving" from one place to another by the shortest way without changing direction or stopping" and defines indirect as "avoiding direct mention or exposition of a subject." So, how can the 'U' be both? It depends on the circumstances. Most of the time the 'U' is very direct; some may even say they lack tact. However, if the 'U' does not wish to share any information the 'U' utilizes indirect methods. Pat Heim's book, In the Company of Women: Indirect Aggression Among Women: Why We Hurt Each Other and How to Stop is an excellent resource that explains how indirect communication can hinder someone from achieving success and harmony in their relationships. This holds true for both women and men. Heims offers straight forward techniques on how to change conflict into cooperation peaceably. Her book also shares how to change indirect communication into direct communication in a non-threatening way.

MOTIVATION TO MAKE A PURCHASE

The 'U's love things that are beautiful, and they love unique experiences. The best thing is to observe what decorative items that are in the 'U's house and find them a gift that goes with their specific style or play it safe, and take them on a new adventure. Do something with 'U' that 'U' has not done previously. Go see a play, an opera, or movie, remembering that they love theatrics. Be creative and surprise your 'U' friend with a night on the town. Just about anything goes. A perfect place to go with the 'U' is the local comedy club!

MOST MISCOMMUNICATIONS

The most miscommunications are with the 'Y'. That is because underneath the 'Y's graciousness is a very serious person. Yes, the 'Y's can laugh, play, and have fun like the 'U's yet they tend to take things literally and are research, factually oriented. 'U's see all that needs to be done to reach their goals and they are driven to do so; meanwhile the 'U' likes to keep things light hearted and mostly superficial. There will only be a few people that the 'U' actually confides in and trusts where they feel safe to really share how they feel and what they are thinking.

HOW TO INITIATE A CONVERSATION

Remember that play is key to the 'U' so when meeting one for the first time, share a joke or funny story as the use of humor is an easy way to connect. Also, keep changing the subject so you don't bore any 'U's. If possible, have quick comebacks to what the 'U' says and keep the subject light hearted. 'U's love to play, so tease, joke, and laugh. The 'U's are great at discussing television shows and the latest movies.

FAVORITE IDIOM

'U's often phrase their thoughts and sentences by thinking or saying, "I hear."

CHAPTER SEVEN: FIRST VOWEL IS 'Y'

Peace is not the absence of conflict, it is the ability to handle conflict by peaceful means."
                    Ronald Reagan, past President of the United States

People who have the first vowel of 'Y' enjoy limitless boundaries and as such are able to see the extremes of a situation. They are able to see both the whole picture as well as the tiniest detail along with the steps necessary to progress from the smallest of minutiae to the whole. Plus, the 'Y' can see parts of the equation that need to be included that totally escape the other first vowels. As such the 'Y' person loves to experiment and take chances. It is an odd occurrence when a 'Y' fails at an endeavor; hence, there is no fear of failure.

Regardless of the type of job, the 'Y' will use his or her natural divergent thinking patterns, coupled with both street smarts and academic learning, to solve creatively the most complex of problems. The 'Y' just thinks differently than the rest of the vowels. Think of Yves St. Laurent and his creative line of clothing. Intelligence in the academic world paired with being street smart makes the 'Y' appear perfect at times. Others forget that the 'Y' has a hard time consistently evaluating others clearly. They think they have a handle on other people; yet, their judgment can be clouded by politics, peer pressure and their own desires. Sentiments can also play a big role regardless of how well the 'Y' has masterfully learned how to hide emotions convincingly.

Due to their precociousness, 'Y's can become quite opinionated firmly believing the way they view things is absolutely the best way possible. Think of Lynn Redgrave as one who definitely has her own opinion and is comfortable expressing it.

Workaholic is too mild a word for most 'Y's; even though, they would disagree as their work is their play and vice-versa. Whether playing or working, the 'Y' will take it to the extremes. When working for someone else, the 'Y' will quietly study where others have made leadership mistakes. They have determined what is needed to progress up the ranks so that when they become the boss, the 'Y' already has a methodology that will minimize errors. The 'Y' has the goal of becoming the boss, and most accomplish that goal even over people with the first vowel of 'O'. 'Y' is definitely a quick study, yet patient.

On the one hand, at times, 'Y's can become overpowering or overbearing in his or her high expectations of others. Since the 'Y' has a lethal tongue and is destructive when mad, 'Y's can be a dangerous enemy once crossed; the 'Y' always retaliates regardless of how long the wait or the number of details needed to execute the perfect plan.

On the other hand, the 'Y' is gracious when satisfied and does his/her best to promote those who please them. The 'Y' has a long memory and moves forward with great force and energy. People with 'Y' as a first vowel are gracious with others. They are thoughtful and considerate to all, so knowing when you have upset one can be difficult. Therefore, a person is often taken by surprise when the recipient of the 'Y's revenge as there is rarely any forewarning.

Being a realist, the challenge for the 'Y' is in the area of spirituality. Again, taking things to the extreme, the 'Y' will either seriously question the existence of a Divine Being or be overly enthusiastic about spirituality, not necessarily religion, investigating an array of beliefs usually outside normal parameters. The 'Y's attribute of patience lets each person realize one has his/her entire life to make a decision in this important area, and thus, is not in any hurry to form a conclusion. Still, know it will be a constant query, regardless of which way the 'Y' eventually chooses.

In dealing with someone who has the first vowel of 'Y' remember:
- Even if you think you've won the argument, you've lost
- Whatever you say will be remembered
- You are always being observed
- They will outsmart you given time
- They are realists
- They are always gracious and can hide true feelings well
- They just know things
- You can be the boss, it just takes time

If you have the first vowel of 'Y', remember:
- Revenge is not always appropriate
- You have many hidden admirers
- Your true friends will be protective of you
- Become your own best friend

- Watch for overindulgence or feeling dissatisfied with the routines of life

LEARNING STYLE

There are three main learning styles, visual, auditory, and kinesthetic. The first vowel of 'Y' indicates that the individual's primary way of learning is auditory, with the secondary modality being visual. Thus, when introducing the 'Y' person to a new concept, it is best to talk about the subject and secondly to give the person a picture and summary of what is being presented. 'Y's need to repeatedly hear something while also being exposed to a visual presentation of the same material new in order to learn best. So, recording the lessons and replaying that tape continuously is an excellent strategy along with having summary notes to review. So, the 'Y's learn by hearing the material that is being presented and secondarily seeing the notes and/or diagrams of the material visually.

LOVE LANGUAGE

Each vowel shows love differently. It is important to understand how the first vowel in the name shows love so that you understand how each vowel feels love. How one shows love is saying how one perceives they are loved. It is wisest to show another person love in the method that they understand the best, and to receive it in the manner that you understand it best. This is similar to when two people who are native speakers in different languages wish to clearly communicate, especially if neither is fluent in the other person's language, yet knows some the language. The clearest communication takes place when one hears their native tongue and then speaks the other one's native language back to them. The same holds true for how we express love, our love language. If we can show love to others in the style that they can easily recognize then we are doing a better job of communicating our feelings.

The 'Y's understand that they are loved when someone shows up for them and lends them their support. 'Y's know people who continually show up for them love them. 'Y's send and receive love in the same style. Thus, when 'Y' continually shows up for you and is there when needed, making time for you, you are loved!

COMMUNICATION STYLE

'Y's are direct, and appreciate getting to the point quickly, just like the 'A's, even if they demonstrate more patience than the 'A's. Similarly, the 'Y's appreciate their time not being wasted. Again, like the 'A', they too often have so much work on their plate that they appreciate people giving summaries of information; however, they also wish to know the all of the details. Just be quick in how you present the information. 'Y's are most gracious always wishing to be sure the other person is okay. However, they can become resentful of anyone who is not gracious to others, and then, a different side of the 'Y' emerges, a side no one really wants to experience. 'Y's have strong opinions about everything, so it's best to stay neutral in your conversations with them as you never know when you'll rile one up where they will wish to even the score later and teach you a lesson. Out of all of the vowels, the person who has the first vowel of a 'Y' is the hardest to know really well as their elegant manners will deceive most. However, being the great detectives that they are, people with the first vowel of 'E' are usually able to figure out the complexities of the 'Y' better than the other vowels.

COMMUNICATIONS

Getting the gracious 'Y' to engage in conversation is easy, as usually, they will approach you to be sure you are feeling included. Topics can range from where their last trip took them, to how they are changing others to see the world from their perspective, or to what creative endeavors have engaged them. They can speak to any topic, so choose one of your choice. However, the 'Y' loves to travel, so asking for advice on how to travel efficiently or where to go on your next vacation is most always a winning topic. 'Y's can also keep up if you choose to jump around in your topic of conversations. They are so completely gracious that you will never know if you are boring them. However, the 'Y' will not forget and do their best to avoid you or pass you off to another person as soon as possible when they see you again.

GIFT PREFERENCES

Gift giving is easy when one remembers that the 'Y' wants something different or creative, and definitely not what everybody else has. Homemade gifts are wonderful as 'Y's are most pleased when they receive something unique or that relatively few people owned. A handmade, one of a kind object, is both appreciated and preferred as they know it took time plus income to make them something.

They wish for their surroundings to be distinctive, so a gift purchased for them while you are traveling would be appropriate. The other great gift for 'Y' is any experience that is out of the ordinary or a trip to a new place as 'Y's love to travel. With their precision memory, the 'Y' will long remember who gave them each gift and also remember to thank the giver once again even years later.

HOW TO MAINTAIN A LONG RELATIONSHIP

One needs to be incredibly tactful and honest and to know when to speak and when to be quiet if you wish to maintain a long-term relationship with the 'Y'. The 'Y' is an active letter so be ready to go do things that take you out of the house. Go ride motorcycles together, go golfing together, do anything that gets you both out of the house together. Plan plenty of activities when you see each other. 'Y's are great at long distant relationships; when you are together, it'll feel like no time as passed at all. Be ready to listen more than talking as the 'Y' is always involved in something that is either brand new or is highly educational. The one thing you definitely wish to do with a 'Y' to keep a long-term relationship going is to remember their birthdays.

IDENTIFIABLE TALENT

The ability to say the right thing at the right time is reserved for the 'Y'. No one beats the 'Y' at knowing how to handle difficult situations. The 'Y's are super at knowing what is really going on behind the scenes and being able to diffuse violent and/or angry people. The 'Y's have been watching others intently while growing up; thus, they have learned from everyone around them what to do and what not to do in various situations.

IDENTIFIABLE CHALLENGE

The 'Y's are like the gatekeepers to fairness and life's issues. Hence, if they feel that you have inadvertently, or on purpose, hurt another individual, regardless of your intentions to do so, it is their job to get revenge and to right the perceived wrongs. It is as if the 'Y' is the police force that hasn't earned a badge. This need for revenge is strong and the 'Y' must fight against the urge to 'make things right' and instead trust the Universe to do just that.

HOW LIFE'S LESSONS APPEAR

Lessons come in three major packages: relationships; finances/resources; and health. Think about it. What lesson have you learned that did not come through one of these methodologies? The good news is that whatever method is used to receive lessons, the other modalities are normally only temporary problems, not permanent ones. So, lessons that come in the other modalities are temporary inconveniences that will right themselves with time. 'Y's major lessons come through finances and how they use their resources. It is important for the 'Y' to plan on using some of their resources for the common good, even if it is simply put in their will that a donation is made to the charity of their choice.

RELATIONSHIP OPERATIONAL STYLE

Y's usually are independent in their relationships. Webster's dictionary defines independent as "free from outside control; not depending on another's authority." It is more difficult for the 'Y' than any other letter to be in a long-term relationship a part of a couple as they treasure their independence. They excel at being a best friend. Good solid friendships can last a lifetime yet being part of a couple is their challenge.

"There is nothing worse than being in a relationship where you feel estranged, distant, unloved, uncared for, or experience never ending tension and conflict" per Larry Shushansky in his book, <u>Independent Enough.</u> Independent relationships eat away at your self-esteem and your overall satisfaction with life. Shushansky examines the myths that our society teaches about relationships. He shares the secrets for creating the kinds of relationships everyone desires and deserves by developing the internal resources needed to engage in healthier relationships.

MOTIVATION TO MAKE A PURCHASE

'Y's are motivated to make a purchase when they can get exactly what they want and/or something that has class and they've not seen the item previously. Something that adds to a current collection is also a motivator. Again, it's a new addition to something that they are already collecting and it has to be something not seen previously. 'Y's don't make a purchase unless they really want the object and it meets exactly what they were looking to buy.

MOST MISCOMMUNICATIONS

The most miscommunications are with the 'U'. That is because underneath the 'Y's graciousness is a very serious person. Yes, the 'Y's can laugh, play, and have fun like the 'U'; yet, they tend to take things literally and are research, factually oriented. They see all that needs to be done to reach their goal, and they are driven to do so; meanwhile, the 'U' likes to keep things light hearted and mostly superficial. It concerns the 'Y' that 'U's aren't serious enough since they don't see the deep side of the 'U' very readily.

HOW TO INITIATE A CONVERSATION

'Y's can talk about anything and everything. They are the gracious hosts and once approached will do their best to make sure that you are the one who feels comfortable. Watch how quickly they pass you off to someone else to speak with as that will let you know the level of their involvement with you and how much they truly care about you. Whatever the 'Y' does, it will be done graciously. Ask the 'Y' about trips they have taken or any unique objects that they have acquired on those trips.

FAVORITE IDIOM

'Y's often phrase their thoughts and sentences by saying "I realize".

CHAPTER EIGHT

"The root of all addiction is the addiction to the pain of not being seen."
                    James Duggan

To paraphrase Arun Ghandi,[1] "We are not who we think we are as we are so much more." We have such dreams when we are children of who we wish to become. That is because we knew what we wanted prior to our cultures, parents, and educational system shaping us into something others wish for us to become. Neimology® Science reaffirms and reminds us of what we knew within ourselves when we were children. We are our names. Our names hold the blueprint of what is planned for our earthly sojourn. Our name even gives us our timing for our yearly focus. Hidden within our full name is the overall reason or purpose for our life and the seven challenges that must be overcome to fulfil that purpose. Our names even provide us the way to solve the problems that come our way if we care to use the secrets that are given to us at birth when we are named. If you would like to know more of Neimology® Science than just the first vowel position in

1   Grandson of Mohandas Karamchand Gandhi, better known as Mahatma Ghandi, who led the Indian independence movement.

a name you can visit www.KnowTheName.com and choose between teaching yourself by reading the other books in the series, or take a class where you are taught the material by the creator of Neimology® Science.

THE TRAIN OF LIFE[2]

"Life is like a journey on a train...with its stations...with changes of routes... and with accidents. At birth we boarded the train and met our parents, and we believe they will always travel on our side. However, at some station our parents will step down from the train, leaving us on this journey alone. As time goes by, other people will board the train; and they will be significant, i.e. our siblings, friends, children, and even the love of our life. Many will step down and leave a permanent vacuum. Others will go so unnoticed that we don't realize that they vacated their seats! Which is very sad when you think about it. This train ride will be full of joy, sorrow, fantasy, expectations, hellos, goodbyes, and farewells. Success consists of having a good relationship with all the passengers... requiring that we give the best of ourselves. The mystery to everyone is: we do not know at which station we ourselves will step down. So, we must live in the best way - love, forgive, and offer the best of who we are. It is important to do this because when the time comes for us to step down and leave our seat empty – we should leave behind beautiful memories for those who will continue to travel on the train of life. I wish you a joyful journey this year on the train of life. Reap success and give lots of love. More importantly, give thanks for the journey! Lastly, I thank you for being one of the passengers on my train."

[2]   Posted on Facebook by Peace Within on 12/22/2018

SUMMARY OF VOWELS IN THE DIFFERENT CATEGORIES

"Circumstances do not define you, they reveal you."
Dr. Wayne Dyer

Sales

A = A good deal, stay on topic, nothing personal, stay on topic

E= bond with sales person, needs to touch and experience the product

I = family involved, benefit to family, ask questions where they can give advice

O= take direction from the 'O' and do what they say, let them take the lead

U= make it fun, explain how the product makes life more fun, complement them, tell jokes, keep them entertained

Y= cause them to feel special, need to explore items being purchased for themselves

Operational style

A =codependent

E= passive aggressive

I = interdependent

O= domineering

U= indirect/direct

Y= independent

Love language
A = do your work for you, harmony, security
E = touch, physical
I = family bonding, inclusive
O= money, finances
U = teasing, playful, surprises, security
Y= support, show up, be there for them

Learning Styles
A = 1st visual, 2nd auditory
E = 1st kinesthetic, 2nd auditory
I = 1st auditory, 2nd kinesthetic
O = 1st visual, 2nd kinesthetic
U = 1st kinesthetic, 2nd visual
Y = 1st auditory, 2nd visual

How lessons appear
A= relationships
E= health
I = relationships, except TRI is finances/resources
O = finances/resources
U = health
Y = finances

Preferred gifts
A = books, classes, practical items, great "regifters"
E = spa day, something for the body, or perfume
I = something off of their list
O = money, or something wanted that is expensive
U = fun experience, new way of being entertained
Y = handmade items, or a trip

Talent
A = great observation skills
E = listening ability
I = including others
O = nurturing others
U = seeing the big picture, creativity
Y = graciousness

Challenge
A = overly sensitive
E = over involvement in other's problems
I = family issues
O = being bossy
U = embellishing their stories
Y = wants revenge

Motivation to make a purchase
A = good deal for the money
E = causes them to feel good about self
I = will benefit family
O = the salesperson provided exactly what they wanted
U = the buying process was fun
Y = the item is unique

Most miscommunications with
A = people with a first vowel of E
E = people with a first vowel of A
I = people with a first vowel of O
O = people with a first vowel of I
U = people with a first vowel of Y
Y = people with a first vowel of U

How to initiate a conversation

A = talk about books read or classes taken; what have they learned lately

E = talk about aesthetics or emotional issues

I = talk about family and what the family is currently doing

O = finances, investments, management challenges of being the boss

U = share entertaining or funny stories

Y = talk about vacations, where to take a trip, or one's goals

Favorite idiom

A = I think

E = I feel

I = I see

O = I know

U = I hear

Y = I realize

AMAZON REVIEWS

for

"KNOW THE NAME; KNOW THE PERSON"

"Once in a while a book comes along that makes you have to stop and think about your life. And this is one of those books. The content is incredible. 'How can she know all this?' you ask as you test the author's guidelines with names of people you know and see how the tenets are on the mark. And then of course you can go from there, and learn about people at work, or why they are so insane in government, or find out about someone you want to date. Simply marvelous and so much fun. Beware though, after you tell your friends about this book, you will be hounded with requests to borrow it (makes a good gift though if you don't like to lend out books). Enjoy."

****

"There is no other book like 'Know the Name; Know the Person'. It's a fascinating book giving insight on how to read a person by understanding the meaning of their name. It's a fun read and makes for great conversation. A must have for everyone's library."

****

"This book posits the science of 'Neimology® Science, the study of names' and is ground-breaking, of potentially historic importance, and it affords broad-spectrum practical application. The empirical research and experience behind it has substantial credibility."

****

"The notion behind the research and this book is that a person's oft-repeated name is initially inspired, releasing a resonance and predictable potential within the person's life expression. The author systematizes how people with names bearing the same initial vowel, initial letter, last letter and middle letters show consistent tendencies. Hence, the resonance of the name demonstrates correlated patterns of conduct due to the structure of the name. This observation is consistent with the ancient knowledge of most cultures' approach to naming children, where the given name 'says it all.' Offering this as a framework for decoding, she does not, for example, claim that every 'John' will be the same, but that every 'John' will share certain traits. Her system explains how and why these traits will be distinct from those shared by persons named Jemal, or James, or Jim. The resulting correlations are nuanced and valuable. Socially, this book can help make interaction with friends and strangers alike far more effortless and productive.

Unlike common 'cookbook' approaches that merely share the meanings of names, the Wyeth system explores the personality traits associated to vowels and consonants, with interpretive weight given to their placement in the name. She enriches the reader with a systematic exploration and many illustrations. The reader is thus equipped with an interpretive framework applicable to any name. She tested the work in many countries who use the English Alphabet and found consistent results with only minor adaptations. This is significant. In addition, she addresses nicknames, changed names, and other permutations involved in naming. In sum, rather than providing a fish to the hungry, she has provided a hook and bait so the hungry can catch fish and eat for a lifetime."

****

"Neimology® Science offers a wealth of very useful applications for anyone who seeks to gain a sense of what lies beneath the surface in other people. The range of applications is broad-spectrum. Among readers who could benefit from Neimology® Science are people in business, sales, counseling, politics, ministry, education, military leadership, and anyone seeking to refine simple interaction among other people in any capacity."

****

"One of the most unique books on human nature."

****

"What's in a name? More than you ever imagined! This book unlocks secrets everyone should know...about others AND themselves. In business transactions, Neimology® Science will save you tons of time, trouble, and even money. On the personal side, it will provide insights to help you connect with others lightning fast. 'Know the Name, Know the Person' is a riveting read and a terrific resource. Fascinating...fabulous...and FUN!"

****

"This book is amazing. I found wealth of knowledge which is useful and helpful in everyday life. Knowing and understanding someone's name sets the parameters of expectations. Once you decode the name, you will never be disappointed. Use it to dating or other partnerships. Highly recommended addition to your library."

****

"Reading this book was an amazing discovery. A door opening to a knowledge that can change the way you live, the way you understand people, the way you interact with people."

****

"What if you had a tool that insightfully and with great accuracy, told you personality traits about a person? This book shows you how you can do just that with eerily accurate results. Learning what is in a name can help you avoid potential conflicts, learn how to meet and connect with someone and improve your ability to sell more of your products. I highly recommend this book if you want to learn more about people and what drives them. Beware though, you may learn something about yourself in the process!"

****

"I'm 8 months pregnant, so I'm sure it will come as no surprise that over the last say... 9 months or so, my husband and I have thought a LOT about names. When picking out our baby's name, we spent countless hours poring through baby name books, baby name websites, and suggestions from friends and family. We carefully scrutinized and argued until we finally came to our decision.

When I picked up Sharón Lynn Wyeth's Know the Name; Know the Person: Decoding Letters to Reveal Secrets Hidden in Names, I thought that I was going to be taking a look at another book about names and their meanings. I was delightfully surprised though when I started reading the book to find it to be about the science of Neimology®. The author of this book spent 18 years of research and observational fieldwork in 49 states and in over 70 countries. What she found were amazing correlations between what someone's name is and how they will be perceived through life - not just by others but by themselves as well.

This book is so interesting, and when I say that it's about the science of Neimology®, I'm not kidding. The book describes with great scientific precision everything you can think of when it comes to the composition of a name - from what the first vowel in your name says about you, to what the last letter of your name implies, to what it means if your name has the letter combination of 'TH' versus 'EL.' I found some of the accuracy of the book fascinating - by breaking down the first vowel of my name, the descriptions of the personality traits that this brings about were eerily spot on."

****

"Through learning the science of Neimology® Science, the author shows her readers how you can learn who to trust. From hiring a new employee to making decisions on who to let handle your money, to even choosing a life partner! I would definitely recommend this book to anyone looking to find out more about either their own name, how to read other people better by understanding their names, or anyone looking for the perfect name for a baby!"

****

"They say that with knowledge comes power. The knowledge I gained from this new understanding of names provided me with a new power to proactively work with people. I can now come from the viewpoint of understanding what drives them at their core, rather than ignorantly misunderstanding their motives."

****

"If you are in sales, this book will provide a wealth of information on how to increase your sales simply by knowing how to effectively work with a client based on their name. Page 83 starts an excellent section on how to win over different buyers based on the first vowel in their name. Do you know how to properly 'treat' an 'A' person, and how would that be different for an 'E' person? What would it cost you in wasted time, money, and frustration if you got it wrong? Buy this book, apply it, and watch your in-person sales soar!"

****

"Great book! I wouldn't say it's 100% accurate but it's very, very close. It's very easy to use and so interesting to put the different pieces and aspects of anyone's name together to read details about their personalities. Some parts are so accurate it's rather disconcerting actually."

****

"Talk about a wealth of information contained in this work-of-art. Curiosity is sparked by Sharón Lynn Wyeth, the author's passion, as she shares a journey of name(s) and proceeds to show us secret treasures she's unearthed about, and FOR us. What An insightful resource & GIFT! Excavating crevices, nooks and crannies, and sharing fascinating discoveries in detail; that others may never have thought to explore. This book is an extremely useful, yet fun tool, that she's made easy for practical daily life application. Her open-mindedness sparks inner and outer observations & conversation. The reader derives that same sense of uplifting exhilaration from her willingness to dive deep, explore new frontiers, and share them with us. There is an adventuresome spirit of buoyancy & knowing, that at any moment new breakthroughs are very possible. It's one of those hard to put down 'thought provoking books.' Loaded with life-changing info. with the potential to change the way we perceive & interact with others - in a profound, positive way. Can barely wait for the author's next book to be published. Highly Recommend, Viva-la-difference!!!"

****

"Delightful, entertaining and right on! Definitely a keeper! Has a lot if information to offer. I most definitely recommend this book."

****

"After hearing Sharón speak on a conference call I was absolutely fascinated in the information she shared and was so pleased to find that there was a book available. I purchased the book immediately and scanned through it - gulping down the information that Sharón has provided in this well-written and informative book. The content provides sufficient detail to allow you to gain insight into who you are and the influence your name(s) and nicknames have on your life! It is based on an incredible amount of research and practical application of what Sharón learnt. I have subsequently been fortunate enough to have a reading with Sharón and it was really a comprehensive view of my journey 'where I came from and the influence of my parents and family and where I am now and what potential is available to me!' Obviously, Sharón has had many years of experience but having heard her reading and scanning the book she has included sufficient detail to enable you to evaluate your own name with confidence!"

****

"So accurate!!!!!!!!!!"

****

"Wow how can this be so accurate! Everyone will think you are psychic."

****

BOOKS IN THE KNOW THE NAME SERIES

Know the Name; Know the Person

This book introduces Neimology® Science: the study of the placement of the letters in a name and how they interact with each other to reveal hidden secrets about one's character. When asked who we are, we respond with our name, as if that says it all. Indeed it does once you know how to interpret a name. This book's focus is on deciphering the personality.

Know the Name; Know the Spirit

This book introduces the spiritual aspects of Neimology® Science from the soul's point of view. It discusses a person's purpose in life and how to find the overarching reason behind a person's birth. This includes how to find the seven lessons in each name.

Know the Name; Know How to Connect

This book introduces the idea of how to use Neimology® Science's first vowel in the first name to show how a person communicates with others so that utilizing this knowledge can assist an individual in improving one's relationships.

Know the Name; Know the Health coming end of 2019

This book introduces the health predispositions hidden in a name. Did you know that what shows up in your first name is what you create from your choices and what shows up in the last name is what you have inherited from your family lineage? Knowing ahead of time where your body is more susceptible to disease can aid a person in avoiding the problems that could appear.

****

Visit www.KnowTheName.com to purchase these books and/or to schedule a private reading with Neimology® Science's creator Sharón Lynn Wyeth.

****

Contact Sharón Lynn Wyeth at info@KnowTheName.com or via the website at www.KnowTheName.com to schedule a personal reading, enroll in an upcoming seminar, and/or purchase her books and CDs.

Printed in Great Britain
by Amazon

64179652R00061